IN CONFIDENCE

A Play in One Act

by

PETER COKE

SAMUEL FRENCH

LONDON

5 of 5

SAMUEL FRENCH LTD
26 SOUTHAMPTON STREET, STRAND, LONDON

SAMUEL FRENCH INC
25 WEST 45TH STREET, NEW YORK
7623 SUNSET BOULEVARD, HOLLYWOOD

SAMUEL FRENCH (CANADA) LTD
27 GRENVILLE STREET, TORONTO

SAMUEL FRENCH (AUSTRALIA) PTY LTD
ELIZABETHAN THEATRE TRUST BUILDING
153 DOWLING STREET, SYDNEY

MADE AND PRINTED IN GREAT BRITAIN BY
LATIMER, TREND AND CO. LTD, PLYMOUTH

MADE IN ENGLAND

CHARACTERS

(in the order of their appearance)

ANGELA FAIRBOURNE
A TOUT
COLONEL EDWARD APLIN
FILIPPO

The action of the play passes on the terrace of the Trattoria del Ponte, in a small square in an unfashionable part of Venice

Time—the present

(The lights are faded on several occasions to denote lapses of time)

IN CONFIDENCE

SCENE—*The terrace of the Trattoria del Ponte, in a small square in an unfashionable part of Venice. Morning.*

The terrace R *is screened from the square by wood lattice-work, creepers, flowers and shrubs in tubs and pots. It has two or three small tables with gay umbrellas. At the back of the terrace is the dark entrance, through a bead curtain, to the restaurant.*

When the CURTAIN *rises, the stage is empty. Faint music comes from a radio inside the restaurant.* ANGELA FAIRBOURNE *enters* L *in the square. She is middle-aged, gay and enchanting. She wears a coloured, close-fitting hat and carries a handbag. She is followed on and is being badgered by a slick, poorly-dressed young* TOUT, *who speaks with a strong Italian accent.*

TOUT. You want nice gondola, Signora?

ANGELA (*crossing to* C) No, thank you very much.

(*The music ceases*)

TOUT (*moving* LC) Very good gondola—take you all place, cheap price.

ANGELA. Not today, thank you.

TOUT. Today I show you famous sights of Venice, yes?

ANGELA. No. (*Hopefully*) Good-bye.

TOUT. You want to see glass factory?

ANGELA. No, thank you. (*Firmly*) Good-bye.

TOUT. I show you nice place to eat.

ANGELA. No!

TOUT. Very clean; speak English; give pot of tea.

ANGELA (*losing patience*) I don't want a pot of tea!

TOUT. What you want, then?

ANGELA. I want you to leave me alone.

TOUT (*moving to her*) But I like you, Signora. (*He touches her*) You very pretty lady.

ANGELA. I'm getting a very angry lady.

TOUT. Pretty lady with pretty clothes, pretty rings, and —(*he looks at her handbag*) pretty bag.

ANGELA (*waving him away*) Go away. *Via!*

TOUT. I "via" if you open bag, pretty lady.

ANGELA. If you don't go immediately I'll call a—(*she glances anxiously around*) someone.

TOUT (*trying a new trick; whining*) I have very ill mama, Signora.

ANGELA. Then go to her.

TOUT (*dramatically*) She die if not eat. (*He touches her bag*) Open bag; give me money buy food.

ANGELA (*frightened*) Take your hand off my bag.

TOUT. Just thousand lire, pretty lady.

ANGELA. No. Go away.

TOUT. When you give money.

ANGELA (*really alarmed*) I'm not going to. Go away— please.

TOUT (*threateningly*) Signora, if you not give money . . .

(*The* TOUT *is interrupted by a bellowed stream of invective which comes from the door of the restaurant*)

COLONEL (*off; bellowing*) *Senta ragazzo! Lasci quella donna in pace o chiamo la polizia!*

(*The* TOUT *glances in fright at the door and turns to flee.* ANGELA *puts her foot out and trips him. He falls heavily*)

ANGELA (*moving* RC) Pretty lady hopes that hurt!

(*The* TOUT *gets up and runs off* L.
COLONEL EDWARD APLIN *enters from the restaurant. He is a well-dressed, military figure, in his late sixties*)

COLONEL (*moving to* L *of Angela*) Forgive my not inter-fering before; I didn't realize what was happening.

ANGELA. It was most kind; thank you so much.

COLONEL. Are you all right?

ANGELA. Perfectly. In the ordinary way I'd have clonked him on the head; but I have something valuable in my bag, so didn't dare risk a tussle.

COLONEL. It's most unusual for such an incident to take place in Venice—especially in this less fashionable district. I trust it hasn't upset you too much?

ANGELA. No, no; I'm used to looking after myself.

COLONEL. You're travelling alone?

ANGELA (*after a glance at him*) Yes.

COLONEL. Then—though you're probably in the mood to beware of strange gentlemen—may I offer you something to restore lost energy?

ANGELA. How very kind!

(*The* COLONEL *gestures to the tables.* ANGELA *moves to the table* C *and sits* L *of it*)

COLONEL (*sitting* R *of the table* C) I suggest a "specialitâ" of this place—fresh peach-juice and gin. (*He calls*) Filippo!

ANGELA. It sounds a little different from my usual mid-morning cup of tea! But I'd love to try it.

COLONEL. Splendid!

(FILIPPO *enters from the restaurant. He is a young, good-looking, smiling Italian waiter*)

FILIPPO. *Colonello?*

COLONEL. *Dammi due bicchieri; la specialitá della casa.*

FILIPPO. *Subito, Colonello.*

COLONEL. *Con molto ghiaccio.*

FILIPPO. *Certamente, Colonello.*

(FILIPPO *exits to the restaurant*)

ANGELA. How clever to speak the language.

COLONEL. Not as well as I should considering I live here most of the year.

ANGELA (*looking at him with increased interest*) How wonderful! Whereabouts?

COLONEL. I have a flat nearby—in a Palazzo overlooking the Grand Canal.

ANGELA (*even more interested*) Am I sitting with a millionaire?

COLONEL (*shaking his head; with a smile*) Merely a retired member of his late Majesty's forces living on a colonel's pension.

ANGELA (*a little crestfallen*) Oh!

COLONEL. But my late father foresaw the plastic age, and my pension's augmented by his forethought.

ANGELA (*her eyes gleaming again*) Ah!

(FILIPPO *enters from the restaurant with two drinks on a tray*)

FILIPPO (*putting the drinks on the table*) *Ecco, Signora.*
COLONEL. *Bene. Grazie.*
ANGELA. Yes, *grazie.* It looks delicious.
FILIPPO. Is delicious, Signora. And the second you find even more delicious.

(FILIPPO *exits to the restaurant*)

ANGELA (*picking up her glass*) Your very good health, Colonel. . . ?
COLONEL. "Edward Aplin." And may you have nothing but pleasant experiences in Venice in future, Mrs . . . ?
ANGELA. "Angela Fairbourne." I'm sure that I shall— (*she gazes admiringly at him*) now.

(*They drink*)

Ummm! I see what he meant about wanting a second.
COLONEL. Shall I order it immediately?
ANGELA. Not unless you wish to sit here till nightfall listening to my very dull life story.
COLONEL. I'm sure it's anything but dull.
ANGELA. A small house in the depths of Wiltshire can't be compared with living on the Grand Canal.
COLONEL. It sounds delightful.
ANGELA. Oh, it is. (*A little pathetically*) But lonely. You see, my husband has—what my beloved daily calls—"gone aloft".
COLONEL (*nodding sympathetically*) Ah. I understand why you used the word "dull".
ANGELA. You mean . . . ?
COLONEL. My wife is also—aloft.

(ANGELA *puts her hand on his arm, and for a moment they sit in silence*)

ANGELA (*musingly*) Of course, it's not the right way to think of it, but I should never have been able to come to Venice if Bertie hadn't . . . (*She glances upwards*) He always maintained, very vehemently, that it "stank".

COLONEL. So did Margaret. Though everywhere except Bournemouth smelt to Margaret.

ANGELA (*lifting her glass*) Let's drink to our less sensitive but—happier noses.

(*They clink glasses and drink happily together*)

COLONEL. How long are you staying in Venice, Mrs Fairbourne?

ANGELA. It rather depends. You see, I've had the most amazing piece of luck.

COLONEL. At the Casino on the Lido?

ANGELA. On the Premium Bonds in London. I've won a thousand pounds.

COLONEL. Impossible!

ANGELA (*excitedly*) That's what I've always thought. But into the pigeon-hole at my hotel last week there suddenly flew one of those common-looking Income-Tax-like envelopes. And inside it said one of my dear little Bonds had won me "one thousand pounds".

COLONEL. How very exciting.

ANGELA (*ruefully*) It's embroiled me in unbelievable trouble.

COLONEL. How?

ANGELA. Well, I immediately wrote off to my friend Mary Truscott, in London, telling her to collect the money, bring it here, and we'd have a gorgeous spree, taking gondolas everywhere and eating scampi every meal.

COLONEL. But surely only you can draw the money?

ANGELA. No; I filled in a form saying I authorized Mary to collect it on my behalf. And enclosed the winning Bond to show I really owned it.

COLONEL. Then why the trouble?

ANGELA. Half an hour ago I got this telegram. (*She takes a telegram from her bag and reads it*) "Idiot. Stop. Can't collect filthy lucre without Bond. Stop. Send immediately."

COLONEL (*puzzled*) I thought you had?

ANGELA. So did I! But in all the excitement I somehow hadn't. (*She takes an envelope from her bag*) It's been sitting in my bag all the week masquerading as general rubbish.

I was on my way to the post office with it when that man accosted me. (*She puts the envelope on the table*)

COLONEL. Ah, so that's the valuable object you have in your bag.

ANGELA. Actually, I meant this gold cigarette-case of Bertie's. (*She takes a gold cigarette-case from her bag*) It is rather valuable, I believe. (*She hands the case to the Colonel*)

COLONEL. Very heavy. It should be. (*He returns the case to Angela*) Isn't it a little unwise to carry it about?

ANGELA (*sadly*) This is probably the last time I shall. (*She puts the case in her bag*) After I've posted my letter I'm going across the square there to the shop of a man with the most lovely long eyelashes.

COLONEL. You're going to sell it?

ANGELA. I must. You see, my friend Molly not having arrived . . .

COLONEL (*interrupting*) Molly?

ANGELA (*a little flustered*) Did I say "Molly"? How stupid! I meant "Mary", of course. (*The excuses tumbling over each other*) Her husband calls her "Molly", and I get muddled occasionally. But her name's "Mary", of course. As I was saying, Mary not having arrived has put me in an awful fix.

COLONEL. Financially?

ANGELA. Yes. When I heard about my fortune I decided to stay on a bit. So instead of paying the hotel bill, I spent the money celebrating. Now the manager's agitating, and owing to my stupidity it'll be several days before Mary arrives.

COLONEL. You must, of course, allow me to tide you over.

ANGELA. You mean lend me money? (*A little too anxiously*) That is what you mean, isn't it?

COLONEL. How much did you hope to get for the cigarette-case?

ANGELA (*almost too pat*) Twenty-five pounds. (*Strongly*) But I wouldn't dream of borrowing it. Let alone from a stranger—(*she beams at him*) however gallant. I can't think what made me tell you about it. Yes, I can! This deceitfully innocent nectar.

COLONEL. I'm delighted it's potent enough to save a

charming innocent from being fleeced. Please allow me to play the gratifying role of St George.

ANGELA (*wistfully*) For all you know, I may only be "playing" the role of the damsel needing saving.

COLONEL. A damsel with a thousand pounds practically in her handbag is no great risk.

ANGELA. Yes, at least I have the proof. (*She picks up her envelope and quickly takes the Bond from it*) Thank goodness that I forgot to post it, now. (*She holds out the Bond*) There it is, you see. Premium Savings Bond K-two-o-two-six-five-eight-one.

COLONEL. I believe without seeing.

ANGELA. No, no; I insist you look.

COLONEL. My dear, however insistent, you can't make me see.

ANGELA (*looking at him in amazement*) You mean . . . ?

COLONEL (*cheerfully*) That I wouldn't know if you were holding a blank paper in your hand.

ANGELA. You're blind?

COLONEL. Completely blind.

ANGELA. I can't believe it.

COLONEL. You couldn't delight me more.

ANGELA. But your eyes—they look perfectly normal.

COLONEL. My particular complaint doesn't affect their appearance, merely their usefulness.

ANGELA. You poor, poor man.

COLONEL. Not at all. I remember the beauty of Venice without having to see its ghastly modern "improvements".

ANGELA. I simply can't believe it.

COLONEL. Many years pretending to be a brave and fearless soldier made me good at counterfeiting.

ANGELA. But you saved me from that tout; how, if you couldn't see?

COLONEL. Loss of one sense has improved all the others.

(ANGELA, *obviously not satisfied, moves her head from side to side in front of him*)

ANGELA. Can't you see at all?

COLONEL. Not even the colour of your hat.

ANGELA (*quickly*) How do you know I'm wearing a hat?

COLONEL (*after only a momentary pause*) It seems likely that a lady from the cool depths of Wiltshire would wear a hat on a hot morning in Venice.

(ANGELA *looks at him, unsatisfied and puzzled*)

Aren't you wearing a hat?

ANGELA. Yes, I am. (*After a brief pause*) A broad-brimmed white straw.

COLONEL (*after a moment*) I'm sure that it becomes you. (*With almost a mocking smile*) I only wish I could see you in it.

ANGELA (*impulsively putting her hand on his arm; ashamed*) I'm a wicked woman.

COLONEL. Why?

ANGELA. Never mind why; I am. (*She replaces the Bond in the envelope and puts it on the table*)

COLONEL. Then I like the sound of wickedness. And insist on subsidizing it to the extent of twenty-five pounds. (*He takes a repeater watch from his pocket*) Now, let me see, what time is it? (*He presses the switch and the watch sounds a quarter to twelve*)

ANGELA. What a gorgeous watch.

COLONEL. Isn't it? (*He holds it out*) Muriel gave it to me when I had the accident.

ANGELA (*sharply*) Muriel?

COLONEL. My wife.

ANGELA. I thought you said her name was "Margaret".

COLONEL (*after only the slightest pause*) Margaret was my first wife; Muriel my second.

ANGELA (*without conviction*) Ah, that explains it. (*She examines the watch*) Gold and enamel; she had excellent taste. How does it work?

COLONEL. You slide this—(*he demonstrates*) and it chimes the nearest quarter.

ANGELA. It's quite lovely.

COLONEL. (*listening to the watch*) Quarter to twelve. Correct?

ANGELA (*looking across the square*) A few minutes after.

COLONEL. Then you've just time to catch your friend with the long eyelashes before he goes to an interminable lunch. Tell him you've changed your mind.

ANGELA. But I can't. I must have the money.

(*The* COLONEL *takes a wad of Italian bank-notes from his pocket, counts out a quantity, feels for Angela's handbag, opens it and puts the notes inside*)

COLONEL. You have the money. Fortunately, I'd just been to the bank.

ANGELA. How very kind and generous. You shall have it back immediately Mary arrives—at the weekend, at the latest.

COLONEL. Suppose you repay my kindness by bringing her here and letting me give you both a "specialità". Shall we say Saturday at eleven?

ANGELA (*rising*) Saturday at eleven it shall be.

(*The* COLONEL *rises*)

And—(*with her hand on her heart*) *grazie, grazie,* for everything.

COLONEL (*smiling*) *Prego.*

(ANGELA *leaves the envelope on the table, picks up her handbag, moves down* L *to exit, but suddenly stops, turns, looks back at the Colonel curiously, and waves gaily. The* COLONEL, *though gazing in Angela's direction, makes no acknowledgement.* ANGELA *waves again, more energetically. The* COLONEL *does not respond.*

ANGELA *shakes her head in a puzzled way, shrugs happily and exits* L. *The* COLONEL *gazes after her, also with a look of puzzlement, then turning to call the waiter, he puts a hand on the table and feels the letter that Angela has left. He picks it up and ponders, then suddenly has an idea*)

(*He calls*) Filippo!

(FILIPPO *enters from the restaurant and moves to* R *of the Colonel*)

FILIPPO. Colonello?

COLONEL. The lady brought me a note. In case it mentions her, I don't want to ask her to read it. Will you do so? (*He hands the envelope to Filippo*)

FILIPPO. *Certamente,* Colonello. (*He takes a letter from the envelope*) *Ecco.* (*He reads*) "My dearest Mary, what a silly-billy I am . . ."

COLONEL. No, stop. That's one of her own letters—is there nothing else in the envelope?

FILIPPO (*taking the Bond from the envelope*) Only a sort of ticket, Colonello.

COLONEL. What does it say?

FILIPPO (*reading*) "Premium Savings Bond. Issued by the Lords Commissioners of H.M. Treasury under Section One of the National Loans Act of nineteen-thirty-nine . . ."

(*The* COLONEL, *exactly as Angela did, shakes his head in a puzzled way, then shrugs happily*)

COLONEL. Well, we'll wait and see what happens on Saturday, Filippo. . . .

(*The* LIGHTS *dim to* BLACK-OUT *to denote the passage of time.*

The COLONEL *exits* L *in the* BLACK-OUT. *Gay Italian music is heard.*

When the LIGHTS *come up, it is a bright, sunny morning.* FILIPPO *is attending to the flowers up* L.

ANGELA *enters hurriedly* L *and crosses to* C. *She has a different handbag*)

ANGELA. *Buon giorno*, Filippo!

(*The music ceases*)

FILIPPO (*moving to* L *of Angela*) Ah! *Buon giorno*, Signora Fairbourne. How pleasant to see you. But are you not early? Il Colonello tell me "eleven o'clock" on Saturday.

ANGELA. I am a little before time. (*With meaning*) Purposely. (*She sits* L *of the table* RC)

FILIPPO (*smiling conspiratorially*) You want secret of peach-juice cocktail, Signora?

ANGELA. No. I want another secret. (*She studies him*) In confidence—you understand me?

FILIPPO (*moving to* L *of Angela; doubtfully*) Well, Signora . . .

(ANGELA *takes her gold cigarette-case from her bag, opens it and holds it out*)

ANGELA. Have a cigarette?

FILIPPO. Thank you, Signora. (*He empties the case*)

ANGELA. I see you do understand. (*She puts the empty case in her bag*) How long have you known the Colonel?

FILIPPO. Oh, long time, Signora—maybe six year . . .

ANGELA. As much as that?

FILIPPO (*gaily*) Maybe even more.

ANGELA. Was he blind then?

FILIPPO. Maybe even more blind, Signora.

ANGELA (*sharply*) More blind?

FILIPPO. I mean, he was bad at finding way. Many time I help him home. Now, no need.

ANGELA. No. (*With a sharp look at him*) He gets about remarkably well.

FILIPPO. Only in the little world he know, Signora. He never go more than his flat, the shops over there, and this *ristorante*.

ANGELA (*acidly*) Then it couldn't have been him I saw near the Rialto Bridge yesterday?

FILIPPO. Near the Rialto Bridge! If he was alone— impossible, Signora.

ANGELA. Whoever it was, was alone all right. And moved off remarkably quickly when I called across the canal. (*She watches him*) Do you know, I have a strong idea —(*she glances off* L, *then continues with hardly a break, but in a slightly louder voice*) that if Regent Street had water flowing down it, it might be almost as beautiful.

(*The* COLONEL *enters* L)

FILIPPO (*puzzled*) Regent Street, Signora?

(ANGELA *nods slightly in the direction of the square* L)

(*He turns and sees the Colonel*) Ah, *buon giorno*, Colonello. (*He moves down* R *and attends to the flowers*)

(ANGELA *rises*)

COLONEL. *Buon giorno*, Filippo. (*He crosses to* L *of Angela*) And *buon giorno*, my dear Mrs Fairbourne.

ANGELA (*suspiciously*) You know I'm here?

COLONEL (*sniffing delicately*) My favourite perfume is "Quelque-fleurs"; I noticed you wearing it the other evening.

ANGELA. Very clever, Colonello.

COLONEL. Merely a perceptive nose, my dear. But it doesn't detect another perfume. Is your friend Molly not with us?

ANGELA (*correcting sweetly*) "Mary." No, my letter was very slow. But I've had a cable; she's joining me tomorrow. (*Miserably*) If I'm still joinable. (*She lays her hand dramatically on his*) Something terrible's happened.

COLONEL. Not so terrible that a gin and peach-juice won't make it better, I'm sure.

ANGELA (*sadly*) I think I'm more in the mood for coffee.

FILIPPO (*moving* C) I make it special—with a little something in it. And for you, Colonello?

COLONEL. Very well.

FILIPPO. I will bring immediate.

(FILIPPO *exits to the restaurant.* ANGELA *crosses and sits* R *of the table* C. *The* COLONEL *sits* L *of the table*)

COLONEL. Now, what's this calamity?

ANGELA. I've had my handbag stolen!

COLONEL (*not quite so sympathetically*) No? Don't say you've lost your gold cigarette-case?

ANGELA. No; fortunately, I'd left that in my evening bag.

COLONEL. So what did you lose?

ANGELA (*mournfully*) The twenty-five pounds in lire you'd so kindly lent me.

COLONEL (*after a slight pause*) How very distressing.

ANGELA. Distressing? It's disastrous! I'd promised to pay my hotel bill, and now I can't. They threaten that either I do by noon, or—*Prisione*.

COLONEL (*a little bitterly*) I shall, of course, lend you more.

ANGELA (*beaming*) I knew you'd say that. And as it's only till tomorrow I gratefully accept.

COLONEL. I'll go to the bank and cash twenty-five pounds as soon as we've had our coffee.

ANGELA. Well—er—as I've been there another three

whole days and entertained rather a lot, I'm afraid—it's quite terrible—that I must ask if you can make it fifty.

COLONEL (*swallowing*) Fifty it shall be.

ANGELA. Bless you! (*She rises*) I'll go and ring the hotel straight away.

COLONEL. If they've waited three days they can wait another half hour. Drink your coffee, which I hear approaching.

(FILIPPO *enters from the restaurant carrying a tray with two cups of coffee which he puts on the table* C)

ANGELA (*resuming her seat*) Yes, of course—how silly of me.

FILIPPO. See if you like, Signora.

(ANGELA *sips her coffee*)

ANGELA. Umm! It is—(*she gestures and dramatically emphasizes every syllable*) mer-vil-i-o-so. Ass-o-lu-ti-ment-ti, mer-vil-i-o-so.

FILIPPO (*delighted*) You speak Italian, Signora.

ANGELA. To be truthful, almost only those two words. (*She beams at Filippo*) But they're all one needs in Venice.

FILIPPO. How kind, Signora, how kind. *Grazie, grazie.*

ANGELA. *Prego!*

(FILIPPO *exits, beaming, to the restaurant*)

What a nice man.

COLONEL. Yes. You must introduce your friend Mary to him. (*A little acidly*) *If* she comes.

ANGELA. If . . . !

COLONEL (*smoothly*) If she comes to this restaurant with you.

ANGELA. We shall give you a meal here to show how much we appreciate your kindness. (*She sips her coffee*)

COLONEL. Such gratitude is most touching. (*Hardly changing his tone*) It makes me less apprehensive about asking you to do something for me.

(ANGELA *chokes over her coffee*)

Are you all right?

ANGELA. Yes, yes—just a little coffee in the windpipe. (*Her voice squeaks in her anxiety*) There's something I can do for you?

COLONEL. There just might be. It depends.

ANGELA (*warily*) On what?

COLONEL. There are some very lovely and amusing paintings by Carpaccio in a church called San Giorgio . . .

ANGELA (*interrupting excitedly*) But I know those Carpaccio paintings. He's my favourite artist. They're wonderful! I spent hours looking at them last week.

COLONEL (*smiling calmly*) I know you did.

ANGELA (*staggered*) You know?

COLONEL. I was there when you were.

ANGELA. Impossible!

COLONEL. I'd taken an English friend to see the Carpaccios. He described a woman he particularly noticed because of her rapt attention before each picture.

ANGELA. But how could you possibly connect her with me?

COLONEL. I didn't. Till just now. Your—(*he imitates her*) "*assolutimenti mervilioso*" to Filippo gave you away. You kept repeating the phrase, in exactly the same way, to the custodian who showed you the Carpaccios.

ANGELA. Well! (*Not at all happy about this explanation*) What an extraordinary coincidence.

COLONEL (*blandly*) Venice is a city of happy coincidences.

ANGELA (*worried*) Oh. But what has this one to do with my—*perhaps* helping you?

COLONEL (*lowering his voice*) Can anyone overhear us?

ANGELA (*after glancing around*) No.

COLONEL. Treat what I'm going to tell you with the greatest confidence.

ANGELA. Yes?

COLONEL. It's come to my ears—(*a little overdoing it*) people are so kind to the afflicted—that a certain Count who lives near the Rialto Bridge, has just bought several paintings for resale.

ANGELA (*suspiciously*) He lives near the Rialto Bridge?

COLONEL. Yes—why?

ANGELA (*worried*) One of your little Venetian coincidences, that's all. This Count's a picture dealer?

COLONEL. Only in a sense. He's an extremely wealthy man who dabbles in Art as an excuse for not entering the family tanning business.

ANGELA. So isn't a great connoisseur?

COLONEL. Precisely; though he has wonderful connections through his family. My informant thinks that one of the pictures—which the Count bought from an impoverished Principessa—is something rather special.

ANGELA. What?

COLONEL (*slowly*) A Madonna painted by Carpaccio.

ANGELA. By Carpaccio? The one we've just been talking about who painted the pictures in the Church of San Giorgio?

COLONEL. Is there another?

ANGELA. But if it were by him this picture would be worth thousands.

COLONEL. Exactly why I'm thinking of buying it.

ANGELA (*slowly*) I begin to see.

COLONEL. Then will you use your eyes for me?

ANGELA (*alarmed*) Me?

COLONEL. Well, it's so easy to deceive the blind.

(ANGELA *starts guiltily and upsets her cup and saucer*)

ANGELA. Oh, I'm so sorry.

COLONEL. What is it?

ANGELA. Nothing, nothing—just the cup upset in the saucer slightly. What exactly do you want me to do?

COLONEL. Others may hear of the picture any time, so I must act quickly. But before I enter into negotiations I want confirmation of the subject, the style of painting, and your view of its authenticity.

ANGELA. You couldn't rely on my judgement.

COLONEL. Your intelligent appreciation of the Carpaccios in San Giorgio makes me think I can.

ANGELA (*sharply*) Why don't you get a proper expert?

COLONEL. Because if it is a Carpaccio, he'd then try and buy it. (*Smoothly*) Of course, I don't expect your advice for nothing. I propose to forget about the small loans.

ANGELA (*hoping to sound disdainful*) With my Premium Bond money they make little difference. I shall go because I'm intrigued.

COLONEL. Good. While you're there, perhaps you'll do something else for me.

ANGELA (*warily*) What?

COLONEL. Take careful note of the other pictures in the room.

ANGELA (*puzzled*) You're interested in them, too?

COLONEL. The Count has a reputation of being crafty. I don't want him to know which painting I'm really after.

ANGELA. You could never get away with pretending to see the pictures.

COLONEL. I could, if you'll memorize every detail of their surroundings.

ANGELA. What sort of detail?

COLONEL. Everything from the time one enters the front door till one reaches the room. Its exact shape and furnishings; where the pictures hang; details of their subjects and colourings; where the window is . . .

ANGELA (*interrupting sharply*) Why?

COLONEL (*blandly*) So that I know what light falls on the pictures. Also who else may live in the house; and whether there are any servants. So that if anyone should come into the room I have an idea of their identity.

ANGELA (*bitterly*) I see I'm going to earn my small loans.

COLONEL (*sweetly*) If you also draw me a map of the house, you will.

ANGELA. How will a map help, if you can't see?

COLONEL. You'll pinprick the lines.

(ANGELA *watches him for a moment*)

ANGELA. If I may say so, it seems a strange and complicated way of buying a picture.

COLONEL. If I may say so, it would be worth far stranger and more complicated efforts if the result is a Madonna painted by Carpaccio.

ANGELA. That's true. (*Briskly*) Well, if we're going to beat the others to the post, I'd better start straight away. What's the Count's telephone number?

COLONEL (*taking a slip of paper from his pocket*) All the particulars are written down here.

ANGELA (*taking the paper*) I'll go and ring him, and arrange an appointment.

COLONEL. How are you going to explain knowing about the picture?

ANGELA. I, too, have an inventive brain, Colonel! (*She rises*) Knowing Italian telephones I shall probably be ages. Perhaps you'll be so good as to arrange my money in the meantime?

COLONEL. I will. And meet you back here.

ANGELA (*pensively*) Thinking it over, fifty pounds may run me a little short. As it's only till tomorrow, could you make it seventy-five?

COLONEL (*wryly*) Seventy-five it shall be.

ANGELA. Thank you *so* much. (*She crosses to* LC *and turns*) Order me a "specialità", will you? I shall need it. I can't think why, but I feel as if I were about to take part in a train robbery!

(ANGELA *exits* L)

COLONEL (*calling*) Filippo!

(FILIPPO *enters from the restaurant*)

FILIPPO. Colonello?

COLONEL. I'm going across to the bank. If the Signora returns before I do, please give her a gin and juice.

FILIPPO. *Certamente*, Colonello.

COLONEL. From the little I heard, you seemed to be getting along remarkably well with the Signora when I arrived this morning.

FILIPPO. The Signora wanted to know—(*he smiles*) certain things, Colonello.

COLONEL. Did she bribe you?

FILIPPO (*cheerfully*) Yes, Colonello.

COLONEL. As well as I do?

FILIPPO. No, Colonello.

COLONEL. So that I should probably approve of the answers you gave.

FILIPPO (*smiling broadly*) I think, Colonello.

COLONEL. Good! (*He smiles and rises*)

 (*The* LIGHTS *dim to* BLACK-OUT *to denote the passage of time.*
  FILIPPO *exits in the* BLACK-OUT. *Gay Italian music is heard.*
  When the LIGHTS *come up, it is evening, and the terrace is lit by coloured bulbs in the lattice-work and discreet table-lamps. The tables are now laid for dinner.*
  The COLONEL *is seated* L *of the table* C, *sipping a drink and waiting impatiently. He takes out his repeater watch and listens in annoyance to it.*
  ANGELA *enters hurriedly* L *and crosses to* R *of the table* C)

ANGELA. Oh, I am so sorry to be late, Edward dear. (*She sits* R *of the table*) But I've had the most terrible afternoon at the airport.

 (*The music ceases*)

COLONEL. Your friend Mary hasn't arrived?
ANGELA. No. Isn't it awful?
COLONEL. Why not?
ANGELA (*without a blush*) Fog.
COLONEL. I haven't smelt fog.
ANGELA. Not here. In London. Never mind, she's sent a cable saying it's clearing, and she'll be here tomorrow, without fail.
COLONEL. "And evermore he said 'tomorrow'."
ANGELA (*innocently*) I beg your pardon?
COLONEL. A quotation by a poet called John Gower.

 (FILIPPO *enters from the restaurant with a drink for Angela*)

FILIPPO (*putting the drink on the table*) I see you arrive, so I bring usual, Signora.
ANGELA. How kind. *Grazie.*
FILIPPO. *Prego.* I start meal in five minutes, Colonello?
COLONEL. Fine.

 (FILIPPO *exits to the restaurant*)

To save time, I've ordered the dinner; I hope you'll approve.

ANGELA. I'm sure I shall; I feel calmer already. (*She takes her cigarette-case from her bag*) A cigarette and I shall be my old self. (*She holds out the case*) Will you have one?

COLONEL. I only smoke cigars, thank you.

ANGELA (*taking a cigarette*) I often think I'd like to, but I'm too cowardly. (*She puts the case in her bag and takes out a lighter*) People will stare at women cigar-smokers. I do myself. (*She flicks the lighter and suddenly holds out the flame in front of the Colonel's face*)

COLONEL (*drawing back sharply*) What are you doing?

ANGELA (*with exaggerated apology*) Oh, I'm so sorry. (*She lights her cigarette*) I was thinking you'd taken a cigarette. (*She puts the lighter in her bag*)

COLONEL. But we were discussing my only smoking cigars.

ANGELA. I was thinking of something else. Something a vet once told me about a litter of Pekingese puppies.

COLONEL. I don't quite follow the connection.

ANGELA (*mischievously*) You would if you knew his theory.

COLONEL. Then you'd better tell me.

ANGELA (*shaking her head*) It would lead to a great deal of discussion, and I know you must be longing to hear about the Count.

COLONEL. I am.

ANGELA. Then the vet can wait. (*She lowers her voice*) Well, it's all going to be much easier than you can have hoped. The room where the pictures are is on the ground floor, on the right, five paces inside the front door.

COLONEL. Yes?

ANGELA. It's furnished as a little drawing-room; I've scribbled down where everything is, and will draw you a proper plan.

COLONEL. Splendid!

ANGELA. There are seven pictures; five hanging and two propped against a sofa. The Carpaccio is about four feet by two and a half, in a gilt frame—rather bashed in the left-hand corner—and hangs so that the bottom of it would be about level with your eyes as you enter the room.

COLONEL. Well done! And your opinion of it?

ANGELA. I just don't know. If I saw it in a gallery, and

it was catalogued Carpaccio, I wouldn't doubt it for a moment. It's exquisitely painted; the Madonna's face glows with ecstasy, and the child is one of the most glorious babies I've ever seen. It's certainly an Italian sixteenth-century painting at the latest, and there's no doubt that it could be by Carpaccio. More I can't say.

COLONEL. You've said enough to make me want it.

ANGELA. I knew you would! (*Happily*) That's why I left a deposit on it.

COLONEL (*aghast*) You did what?

ANGELA. You know the seventy-five pounds you gave me yesterday?

COLONEL (*apprehensively*) Yes?

ANGELA. Well, when I went to settle my hotel bill last night, I'm blessed if it wasn't full of errors.

COLONEL. So you refused to pay?

ANGELA. Of course. I went out early this morning, and they still hadn't got it right. So I happened to have the whole seventy-five with me when I visited the Count.

COLONEL (*ominously*) Go on.

ANGELA. When I saw the Carpaccio, I knew you mustn't miss it. So I paid the seventy-five as a deposit.

COLONEL (*sighing heavily*) I see. (*Suddenly*) You didn't give my name?

ANGELA. Of course not. I'm not nearly so silly as you imagine, my dear Colonel Aplin.

COLONEL (*grimly*) I'm realizing faster and faster that you're the exact opposite, my dear Mrs Fairbourne.

(FILIPPO *enters from the restaurant*)

FILIPPO. I bring mussels, now, Colonello?

ANGELA. Mussels! How gorgeous. Yes, quickly.

(FILIPPO *exits to the restaurant*)

(*Tentatively*) My bill's sure to be made out correctly when I get back tonight.

COLONEL (*resigned*) I'll get you another seventy-five in the morning.

ANGELA (*innocently; smiling*) Another hundred and seventy-five.

COLONEL. I beg your pardon?

ANGELA. I've been most dreadfully extravagant. I've seen a shop with the most divine little bit of mink. Only a hundred pounds—ridiculously cheap. I've reserved it, and I want to pay and fetch it as soon as the shop opens so that I can surprise Mary in it when I meet her. Can you possibly manage the extra hundred?

COLONEL (*warningly*) My dear, I know you're being useful to me, but I really . . .

ANGELA (*interrupting*) Of course, if you'd rather not, it doesn't matter in the slightest. It just means I shall have to be busy trying to find someone else kind enough. (*With eyes wide*) Goodness knows when I shall have time to draw the plan of the Count's house.

COLONEL (*with a deep sigh of resignation*) You shall have the hundred and seventy-five.

ANGELA. You are a dear! Though I was absolutely sure you would be.

COLONEL. Why?

ANGELA. Because of my vet and the Pekingese puppies. You *must* remind me to tell you about it.

(FILIPPO *enters from the restaurant carrying a steaming dish of mussels*)

Ah! The mussels. Done with plenty of garlic, I hope?

(*The* LIGHTS *dim to* BLACK-OUT *to denote the passage of time.*

ANGELA *and the* COLONEL *exit in the* BLACK-OUT. *Music is heard.*

When the LIGHTS *come up, it is early morning. The chairs are stacked on the tables and* FILIPPO, *in his shirt-sleeves, is sweeping the terrace. A bucket is* LC.

The COLONEL *enters quickly* L, *carrying a light coat and a suitcase*)

COLONEL. Filippo?

FILIPPO (*moving to the Colonel*) Colonello. (*He guides the Colonel round the bucket* LC *to the table* C) Mind the water! But how early you come.

COLONEL. And in a hurry. (*He puts his case on the ground*

RC *and his coat on top of it*) So sit down with me and pay careful attention.

> (FILIPPO *puts down his broom, takes two chairs from the table* C, *sets them* R *and* L *of the table, then sits* L *of the table*)

(*He sits* R *of the table*) I have to go to England unexpectedly. I'm catching the ten o'clock plane this morning.

FILIPPO. Something is wrong, Colonello?

COLONEL. I hope not! (*He takes a wad of lire notes from his pocket*) Now, there are one or two things I want you to do for me—(*he hands some notes to Filippo*) if you will.

FILIPPO. I shall be pleased. (*He counts the notes*) Very pleased.

COLONEL. I haven't let any of my friends know that I'm going, so you'd better not know. Or have seen me this morning.

FILIPPO. I saw you last yesterday afternoon, Colonello.

COLONEL. Good. In case I may be—delayed, I've packed two bags and left them at the station. (*He hands Filippo a cloakroom ticket*) Here is the receipt. If I want them I shall write asking you about your two "children".

FILIPPO. I will then immediately send the bags.

COLONEL. Without advertising the fact. Next—this note. (*He hands a letter to Filippo*) It's for Signora Fairbourne.

> (ANGELA *enters quietly up* L, *unseen by the others*)

I have an idea she'll come here this morning . . .

ANGELA (*crossing to* C) Your idea is perfectly correct, Edward.

FILIPPO (*rising*) Signora!

ANGELA. Well, this is a surprise. I got up at dawn to see the fish-market. But what on earth are you doing here so early, Edward?

COLONEL. Leaving you a note, my dear.

ANGELA. Then how fortunate that I returned from the fish this way. (*She sits firmly* L *of the table* C) It'll be so much nicer to hear its contents than read them.

COLONEL. I only have a short time, but may I offer you breakfast in the shape of a cup of coffee?

ANGELA. How kind.

COLONEL (*to Filippo*) *Due caffelatte.*

FILIPPO. It cannot be quick so early, Signora.

ANGELA (*gaily*) *I'm* in no hurry.

(FILIPPO *smiles at Angela and exits to the restaurant*)

Now, what's this intriguing note, Edward?

COLONEL. Poor Muriel's had a fit.

ANGELA. I thought poor Muriel was beyond having fits.

COLONEL. You're confusing her with Margaret.

ANGELA. I must be.

COLONEL. Although we're separated, I'm still very fond of Muriel. As we're apparently to be separated for good, I'm flying to her bedside this morning.

ANGELA. So that's why you're taking the ten o'clock plane.

COLONEL (*surprised*) You know?

ANGELA (*innocently*) Another of your strange Venetian coincidences. I went to the booking place—to check when my friend Mary was arriving—and there on the outgoing list was your name.

COLONEL (*acidly*) Was your friend Mary's name on any incoming list?

ANGELA. Yes. Isn't it lovely? She'll be here tomorrow.

COLONEL. I thought she was due this morning?

ANGELA (*beaming*) Another little delay. (*Distressed*) I am sorry you're going to miss her.

COLONEL. So am I.

ANGELA. And what terrible news that you've also missed the Carpaccio Madonna.

COLONEL (*after a little pause*) I—don't quite understand.

ANGELA. Surely you've heard?

COLONEL. What?

ANGELA. That it's been stolen. Apparently the Count found it missing when he got back about two o'clock this morning.

COLONEL. No!

ANGELA. Some one got him out of the way with a fake message about having a picture to sell far in the country. Then forced the latch on the window of the very room the Carpaccio was in, and went off with it.

COLONEL. How do you know all this?

ANGELA. It's in the stop press.

COLONEL (*shrugging*) Oh, well! We must just hope that it wasn't a genuine Carpaccio.

ANGELA (*indignantly*) I shall be very angry if it isn't, after all my trouble.

COLONEL (*slowly*) I don't quite follow you, my dear.

ANGELA (*smiling sweetly at him*) Don't you, Edward? Well, let's say that I'm silly enough to have an idea who the—present owner of the Carpaccio is.

COLONEL. In that case, you must go the police, my dear.

ANGELA (*naïvely*) They wouldn't help me buy my little bit of mink.

COLONEL. I was under the impression that I'd already done that.

ANGELA (*pensively*) I really must learn Italian before I come to Venice again; lack of it causes such misunderstandings. When I got back to the fur shop I found it wasn't a hundred pounds the mink cost, but two hundred.

COLONEL (*adamantly*) No, my dear!

ANGELA (*wide-eyed*) You won't lend it to me—till Mary arrives?

COLONEL. No!

ANGELA (*cheerfully*) Oh, I think you'd better, Edward.

COLONEL. Why?

ANGELA. Because a hundred is ridiculously little when one thinks of the price of a Carpaccio.

COLONEL (*politely*) You seem to suggest that I'm concerned in its loss.

ANGELA (*horrified*) I'd never dream of suggesting anything so horrid, Edward. (*Ruefully insinuating*) But there are certain evil-minded people who might possibly think so if they knew how you first got me under a strong obligation by lending me a paltry twenty-five pounds . . .

COLONEL (*interrupting smoothly*) Plus another seventy-five pounds, together with substantial expenses; followed by a further hundred and seventy-five pounds. Not so paltry when one considers what those same evil-minded people might call the cock-and-bull story that supported your requests for the loans.

ANGELA (*indignantly*) England's Premium Bonds cock-and-bull!

COLONEL. There was never any proof that you'd actually won.

ANGELA. But I was most careful to leave the winning Bond and my letter to Mary so that you could have them checked.

COLONEL (*charmingly*) There was a Bond and a letter, certainly. But was it a *winning* Bond, and is there such a person as Mary?

ANGELA (*equally charming*) If you'd any doubts—which is absurd—it might be considered even more probable that the loans were merely to trap me into doing what you wanted.

COLONEL. You have a wonderful imagination, my dear.

ANGELA (*sweetly*) Haven't I? It's even suggested that our first meeting wasn't as much due to chance as I supposed. That you sat in the Carpaccio church until you saw some-one possible. And that you then arranged for a tout to drive her here, where you sat waiting.

COLONEL. How absurd!

ANGELA. Isn't it? As absurd as the idea that you've known for some time about the Madonna, but didn't want to be seen near or at the house, because you might be recognized from previous—exploits. So pretended to be blind. Which attracted confidence and sympathy, and gave a reason for asking someone else to spy out the land.

COLONEL. You think I only pretend to be blind?

ANGELA. Gracious, no! I'm only saying what some people might think. Especially if they knew my vet.

COLONEL. You must tell me about him.

ANGELA. Well, we thought one of the puppies might be blind. I rang the vet, and he told me to light a match just in front of its eyes.

COLONEL. As you lighted your lighter in front of mine?

ANGELA. Did I? In that case all I had to do was watch whether your pupils contracted, and I'd know for certain whether you're blind or not.

COLONEL (*acidly*) What a pity there's no such simple way of knowing whether Mary and the money exist or not. (*He takes out his watch and listens to it*) What I do know, though, is that the friend who's guiding me to the airport is waiting at the corner of the square. Do you see my coat anywhere? (*He rises*)

ANGELA (*rising*) It's on your suitcase, here. (*She crosses to the case and examines it with interest*) Not a very big suitcase. (*With meaning*) I hope you've got—everything you need in it.

COLONEL. I think so.

ANGELA. I really wouldn't have thought it large enough. Long enough, certainly. (*Puzzled*) But not wide enough, surely? (*Happily realizing*) But, of course. If one—(*she makes a rolling-up gesture*) rolls things up, they fit in wonderfully, don't they? Yes, I'm sure it's large enough, after all.

COLONEL. Then perhaps you'll be kind enough to give it to me.

ANGELA (*standing between the Colonel and his case*) You know, it's odd—(*she beams innocently at him*) but I don't feel kind this morning. I don't think I shall give it to you.

(*There is a long, silent battle of stares*)

COLONEL (*realizing he is trapped, but still hoping to escape*) With the cooler weather coming, I'm unhappy about you not having your mink. But I shall miss my plane if I wait to get you a hundred pounds.

ANGELA (*sweetly*) Maybe you're even more likely to miss it if you don't.

COLONEL (*after a moment's thought*) Then—for Muriel's sake—I shall let you have most of the money I'd hoped to arrive in England with. (*He takes out his wallet and counts out twenty five-pound notes*) Here you are. (*He holds out the notes but lets go of them before Angela takes them, so that they fall to the ground*)

ANGELA (*bending and collecting up the notes*) Oh, you've dropped them.

COLONEL. I thought you had them.

(*The* COLONEL *steps forward and collides with* ANGELA. *She stumbles and there is a slight muddle*)

Oh, I'm so sorry.

ANGELA. It's all right.

COLONEL. I didn't hurt you?

ANGELA. No, no.

COLONEL. You have the money?

ANGELA. Thank you very much. (*She picks up his coat*) Here is your coat and suitcase.

(ANGELA *helps the* COLONEL *into his coat*)

COLONEL. Thank you. (*Genuinely*) I wish I hadn't to go. Very much so. I shall miss your refreshing and enchanting company, Angela dear.

ANGELA (*touched*) How very charming. I shall miss you, too, Edward dear. (*She gazes at him*) I *do* hope those evil-minded people are right about your eyes, and that you *can* see . . .

COLONEL. I hope they're wrong, and that you have got a friend called Mary who's going to arrive with a thousand pounds.

ANGELA. Probably we shall each know by the next time we meet. For of course we must—even if it's only so that I can repay the loans.

COLONEL. I shall look forward to seeing you for two reasons. You'll find my bank address in the note. In the meantime—good-bye, my dear Angela.

ANGELA. Good-bye, Edward dear. (*She puts her hand into his*)

(*The* COLONEL *kisses Angela's hand, picks up his suitcase and exits* L. ANGELA *sits* R *of the table* C *and looks after him with an enigmatic smile.*

FILIPPO *enters from the restaurant carrying a tray with two cups of coffee*)

FILIPPO. Il Colonello has gone, Signora? (*He puts the coffee on the table* C)

ANGELA. Yes.

FILIPPO. How sad.

ANGELA. Yes; it means I shall have to pay for the coffee. Never mind. (*She opens her handbag*) Never mind. How many cigarettes to tell me the truth, Filippo?

FILIPPO (*smiling broadly*) Many, many, Signora.

ANGELA. Then I shan't be able to hear it—(*she scuffles about in her bag*) as I don't seem to have even one. (*She turns the contents of her bag on to the table*) That's very odd. I know I had my gold cigarette-case when I came here. (*Suddenly*) Quickly! Stop the Colonel immediately!

FILIPPO. He is gone, Signora. But I am sure he would not take it.

ANGELA. Are you! You wouldn't be if you'd seen the little scuffle about the money he managed to arrange.

FILIPPO. But Il Colonello has much money, Signora.

ANGELA. Yes, I think it was more as a little revenge. (*Thoughtfully*) The cunning old . . . (*She smiles happily*) Fortunately, two can play at that game.

FILIPPO. What game, Signora?

ANGELA (*lowering her voice*) Well, absolutely in confidence, Filippo—I benefited from the scuffle, too.

> ANGELA *takes the Colonel's repeater watch from her pocket and smiling seraphically, holds it near her ear, and causes it to ring out the time as—*

the CURTAIN *falls*

FURNITURE AND PROPERTY PLOT

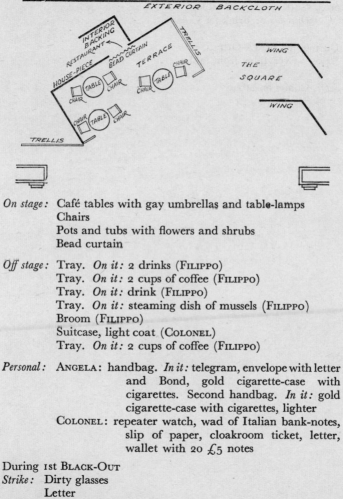

On stage : Café tables with gay umbrellas and table-lamps
Chairs
Pots and tubs with flowers and shrubs
Bead curtain

Off stage : Tray. *On it :* 2 drinks (FILIPPO)
Tray. *On it :* 2 cups of coffee (FILIPPO)
Tray. *On it :* drink (FILIPPO)
Tray. *On it :* steaming dish of mussels (FILIPPO)
Broom (FILIPPO)
Suitcase, light coat (COLONEL)
Tray. *On it :* 2 cups of coffee (FILIPPO)

Personal : ANGELA: handbag. *In it :* telegram, envelope with letter and Bond, gold cigarette-case with cigarettes. Second handbag. *In it :* gold cigarette-case with cigarettes, lighter
COLONEL: repeater watch, wad of Italian bank-notes, slip of paper, cloakroom ticket, letter, wallet with 20 £5 notes

During 1st BLACK-OUT
Strike : Dirty glasses
Letter

During 2nd BLACK-OUT
Strike: Coffee cups

Set: Cutlery, etc., on tables
    On table c: drink for Colonel

During 3rd BLACK-OUT
Strike: Everything from tables

Set: Chairs on tables
    Bucket (LC)

LIGHTING PLOT

Property fittings required: table-lamps, fairy lights

Exterior. A terrace. The same scene throughout
THE MAIN ACTING AREA is C of the terrace
THE APPARENT SOURCES OF LIGHT are, in daytime, bright
sunlight; and at night, table-lamps and fairy lights

To open: Effect of morning sunshine

Cue 1   COLONEL: ". . . on Saturday, Filippo."   (Page 10)
           Dim LIGHTS *to* BLACK-OUT *to denote passage of
           time*

Cue 2   Follows above cue   (Page 10)
           Bring up LIGHTS *for bright sunshine effect*

Cue 3   COLONEL: "Good!"   (Page 18)
           Dim LIGHTS *to* BLACK-OUT *to denote passage of
           time*

Cue 4   Follows above cue   (Page 18)
           Bring up LIGHTS *for evening effect*
           Bring in fairy lights and table-lamps

Cue 5   ANGELA: ". . . garlic, I hope?"   (Page 21)
           Dim LIGHTS *to* BLACK-OUT *to denote passage of
           time*

Cue 6   Follows above cue   (Page 21)
           Bring up LIGHTS *for early morning sunshine
           effect*

EFFECTS PLOT